DOWSING FOR LIGHT

Poems by

Kennette Harrison

Elk River Review Press

DOWSING FOR LIGHT

First Edition

Library of Congress Catalog Card Number
99-72278

ISBN 0-9659751-3-4

Poems in this collection have appeared in *Cumberland Poetry Review, Alalitcom, The Mind Under Thorns, Elk River Review, Cotyledon, Journal of Poetry Therapy, Nimrod Awards X, New Plains Review, Octoberfest V, Mind Matters Review, Do I Know You?, The Sucarnochee Review, Phoenix, Piecework, Redbud, Red Mountain Rendezvous, Southern Humanities Review, Aura Literary/Arts Magazine, The Sampler, Changing Men, The New Laurel Review, ByLine, Poem, Amaryllis, Kitchen Without Precedent,* and *Helmsman.* "*The Old Woman Says, Bring Me Garlic and Grandchildren*" received a Hackney Literary Award in 1990, funded by Mr. Cecil Hackney and sponsored by Birmingham-Southern College.

Cover design: Kennette Harrison

Elk River Review Press
J. William Chambers, Editor
606 Coleman Avenue
Athens, AL 35611-3216

ACKNOWLEDGMENTS

This volume of poetry is the culmination of a life blessed with supportive family members, fellow writers, teachers, editors, and my publisher, John Chambers. My parents Doug and Jo Harrison, living in their Gingerbread Farm get-away deep in piney woods; my poet/editor friends Bonnie Roberts, Sandra Soli, Carolyn Coleman, Sue Starkey, Chris Farman, Ginny Gilbert, and Susan Luther; and my teachers Bill Gammill, Dr. Lynette Wert, Dr. Anne Whaling, and Dr. Loree Rice have all been wordsmiths whose contributions I have valued.

Deep appreciation is felt for the Creative Studies Department of the University of Central Oklahoma where mentoring instructors and visiting artists promoted in me a passion for writing which has not waned. I was often reminded not to take things too seriously by the joyful Betty Shipley, who served briefly as Poet Laureate of Oklahoma before she departed for poet heaven.

I will not forget the forum provided to me and other writers by the historical and literary journals which first published my poems. To individuals, organizations, and groups that have supported my poetic endeavors or have provided a network for other writers, I say a heartfelt "thank you."

To the poets past and present who have inspired, consoled, strengthened, and challenged me, I have only the little bit of light I have dowsed to share in return. Poems for *Dowsing for Light* have been revised with particular help from my friend and story-warrior peer Bonnie Roberts, author of *To Hide in the Light*. Besides our addiction to light, we are both drawn to the hilarious of life and do take laughter seriously. As a thank you to Lucille Clifton and R. T. Smith, wonderful poets who have befriended and encouraged me, I pass your kindness on to other writers. Annie Dillard, wherever you are, *Pilgrim at Tinker Creek* abides with me.

FOREWORD BY SANDRA SOLI

Introducing poems by Kennette Harrison is difficult without saying, "Look here!" and "No, look here!" Favorite passages leap from the page with their own energy, as does my own treasury of hours shared with this poet in amiable conversation about things both ordinary and amazing: a line break, motion within a stanza, or the moment of *if* that rises from a beautiful density of language, deep and mysterious as the piney woods of her childhood memory. "Nothing is ordinary," says Harrison, "when you can hold it with your eye."

Landscapes, real, remembered, or imagined, are realms a poet might play in. Wesley McNair says that poetry is the art of disclosure, but that a poem must also conceal, saving itself for a final unfolding. Poems by Kennette Harrison unfold not so much as disclosure, but as meditation on what might be true, as well as what *is*.

This first collection reveals a well-grounded poet whose clear obligato voice invokes the generational chorus of dauntless women looking over her shoulder. Do not be misled. Harrison is a woman of the South, but these are not primrose path verses, nor Gothic amusements. Rather, they are hands-in-the-meatloaf poems that challenge readers to enter the sensual *paso doble* of risk that inhabits her word-dance, like "the bright coin / of love and death."

The poetry gives itself to us in lush, often elegiac, cadences. Then comes the swift *ah!* as we remember, or fancy that we remember, the flutter of bird-wing: a moment she has conjured from the depths of experience.

Humor comes unbidden. "I'm a good-looking ugly woman," she asserts with Lucille Clifton's jubilant self-understanding. Like Clifton, Harrison knows that acceptance is possible only after self-forgiveness. Above all, she honors and forgives the past as she "dowses for light," exploring unknown image territories where "quest" and "questioner" become one.

The world that inspired these poems is flawed, yes, but Harrison would not ask for a perfect one as inspiration. "What pulses in stone" may cause a heart or foot to stumble, but always the larger Self pays attention. If acceptance of the past is relevant here, so is answering the call to change. In response to lines by R. T. Smith, she covenants: "I will be the one mourner / who will know you by your colors / and at your burning / be transformed."

Harrison says that she is not a religious poet; yet, the "journey mercies" she speaks of demonstrate the spiritual dimension central to this work as she moves "toward something that makes me / want to touch it like a newborn's head."

In celebrating paradox, Harrison reminds us that loss and longing are intertwined with joy in the ivied garden of the spirit. Through these poems, a gate opens, inviting readers into a "garden of survival. . . a garden of grand design," where even doubters can banish darkness by "dowsing for light." And "what if music happens?"

CONTENTS

I THE HEART'S DRY HOLES

II THE LAYING ON OF HANDS

III THE PROMISE CURVE

THE HEART'S DRY HOLES

over the rising dark

a trembling twig

dowsing for direction

Grandpa witched for water weekdays

and Sundays under the steeple pursued
some deep history of soul from his pulpit
then stepped down, laying on hands
knowing the heart's dry holes
piercing through them
a thousand oracles below their desert
trusting his divining rod, believing
the promise curve, quivering
and alive with discovery.

Mother, tired of drinking bitter
iron water from our well, sliced
a green sap branch from the gum tree
and criss-crossed our land
aproned, flour on her hands
unconvincing water witch.

I drink her sweet water
until withered by unbelief
I scoff, yet never cease reading stories
of a captain stanching blood
on the battlefield, of crystals
spun on a string twirling toward
a body's pain, of a mystic spinning
tales that Stonehenge is a place
of underground streams dowsed by ancients.

Spun into my present on a twist of doubt
and a strand of faith, I take a knife
to the sweet gum tree beside my house
and cut a young branch, Y-shaped.
Over the earth I walk with it
expectant, two hands and a dream.
What if music happens?

Thomas Redux - brought back

Doubting thomas

I don't want to probe the violated palm
of a resurrected Christ with my doubting.
Just show me.
I too have experimented
with the crucible of loss
and only want to read my future
while I'm waiting for incoming light
waiting for the intelligence of childhood.

I'm a charitable critic, not selling evolution
in fact, espousing only minimal fiddling with genes.
My library has no works which include
collected regret or encyclopedias of evil.
I have no wicked companions, only questions
   shall I kneel facing westward
   or follow the light in the East
   hark to the minaret
   or sweet hay manger?

Rosary beads roll through devout hands
smooth as boxcar bearings carrying cattle
to slaughter, Jews to Dachau, me to my end
in the sullied, unsweet hay.

Show me a yellow labyrinth
      a tenth dimension
      a parallel universe
         a time warp
            strings
          wormholes
       and hyperspace.

Give me that rib missing from Adam
and I will dowse for direction.
Give me the hole in your palm.

God's Day in the Downtown Mission

If I could pull faith like taffy
pull until silver spindles light the clear brown
if I could make the last stretch
against resistant crystals
before they harden into something sticking
to my teeth like God's Day in the Downtown Mission.

"Grease your hands," Mother said, "or they'll stick."
The oily signs: *Do Not Curse, Do Not Spit*
in God's House.

I play hymns with slippery fingers
keep singing, ignore the man convulsing under the pew
who will rise like boiling sugar to spatter the air
with Shakespearean English from the Good Book
dripping in his hands.

When a city bus crashes through the half-hinged
double doors and no one turns to look, I sing
All Hail the Power, loud. Lord, Lord
we have all come from the soft boil
to hard crack stage, tester drops in the cup
that overflows with God's grace
and free soup after.

On the occasion of my bad breath

my carnal breath, my bus toilet
under the bridge vagrant breath
it should be noted that I graduated
from the Church of Roadkill, and
I have suffered from God's grenade.
I carry spiritual shrapnel
too dangerous to remove.

The beloved flesh
of this romantic animal me
has made birds weep, has been
saint chasing and boundary breathing
has inhaled every shade of down
blues being the favorite
  stale cigarette and last beer blues.

Can you spare a dollar?
I've been through the war
and I can prove it. I have a harp
in my heart
if you care to look, if you'll
come a little closer.

Stigmata

The garden sun
which rose
to spend its twilight
on a silver kiss
clangs down
behind thick crosses
on the hill.

From beyond
the reach of stars
comes the Father's message
fiery as a comet tail
"My Son
in whom
I am
well pleased...."

The mind under thorns
walks crab-like
from the question *why*
as absolution clots
on hands
feet
the pierced side.

Father, forgive.
They know not what
in taverns
their fat tongues
grieve.

Kicking the Preacher: Thirty Years Later While Dividing My Peonies

I practiced for baptism, held air in my lungs like treasure
put my face two inches under the bath water because I knew
God wanted me to be born again, immerse myself
but I was afraid of water, ashamed
before the guppies in my aquarium
the baptistry behind glass
high above the choir
and the congregation
watching.

I pinched my nose, practicing—will my dress float
over my head, will they see my panties, my sins
and what if the preacher in his wading boots
and ballooning jellyfish robe should drop me?

I've seen jellyfish, Man o' War washed up on the beach
tentacles that could stretch from the baptistry
to the front pew.
We wore boots and jumped on them till they popped.
Is that a sin?
If I sink to the bottom
will the preacher step on me?

I rise up, kicking the preacher under water, breathing out
the Holy Spirit in liquid testimony, understanding betrayal
at the table, in the garden, lives torn like divided roots
their underground intimacy interrupted after thirty years

Christ, his peony head staked up, too petal-heavy
to lift to the Father—the thin mother stem collapsing
water flowing from the side. Son of God
anthers and stamens wilting
the cloned beauty Christ
surrendering to seed.

Every day I want to move death

to the side of the road
possums, raccoons, even skunks.
I want nothing ended

so I speed past seven days
of Genesis satisfaction
zip by gritty promises of Exodus
Moses, denied and hitch-hiking

make the slow climb of Revelation
to witness justice by the mile
swerve to miss roadkills
their last chapter read

can't resist glancing
into my rearview mirror
where they always move
quick—like lightning

each after-image chronicled
in the dark at the back
of my living eye.

The Aromatic Christmas Jesus

At this smug fireplace, stocking bright
bygone music Handels through the room
and there is elixir of hay and manger
no cross, no nails, but a tree, redolent
with cedar, fir, or pine; hung with pomanders
of cinnamon, cloves, and nutmeg;
decorated with all the birds of China.

Nativity hover of frankincense and myrrh
perfumes the air, postpones Armageddon
delays it with fragrances which sing us
on our migrations through another year

while in low cloud over downtown Toronto
dazzled birds mistake lighted windows
where someone mops the floor at night
for crystal stars that guide
and flocks of songbirds, propelled by light
collide with skyscrape glass
then plummet to sidewalks
where someone sweeps them up
before the dawn, bygone music.

Bless us in our journeys
aromatic Christmas Jesus
nutmeg eggnog Jesus
mulled wine, cinnamon
clove Jesus, Christmas
pomander, crystal star
Jesus, mangered essence
songbird Jesus, potpourri
sidewalk-sweeping Jesus.

Riding the Nightmare of Her Cries

I

Where is this child who is like a rose
which is like a little girl
granddaughter

hidden away by her father
somewhere sleeping like breath
which is the come and go

of dream, murmuring mama
like a prayer which is
the full breast waiting

what we all want
when we cannot find
where we are

where life without mother
is the place we are in
when we are lost

and we fold up
like this child
in pink blanket faith

letting amnesia
launder everything
belonging to pain.

Where is this child
whose room my daughter
has shut and locked

like a true believer closes
the Bible, secure the words
will reappear when next needed.

ii

You, my daughter, leave the insoluble
to grace or miracle, leave your
stolen baby's heart to beat

somewhere, like a trusted machine
noisy enough to outvoice
the slow scream

while amnesia
becomes the way
you live

hiding the photo album
the baby book, storing the toys
in boxes taped tight

forgetting the rocking horse
which might buck
and squeal

reins held tight, like he tethered
you before he ran
with your daughter

circus horse going nowhere
black eye he gave you healed
handprint on your neck faded

but his rope there now
the chafing noose
of her absence

the three of you rocking
like the last Christmas
you saw her, rocking

together, when you were
playing Mrs. Santa
the three of you

rocking faster and faster
while he jerked the reins
until you flew into a wall

where he beat your head
holding your hair like
a mane, his fist

clutching the knotted rope
of the nightmare
where she cries

mama
  mama
     ma
      ma

Bringing Blood

"If they bleed, they're alive," the vet says
her scalpel scraping, making a red stream
down the colt's trembling leg.
"Wound's too old to stitch
only come apart later
waste your money."

And I remember how raw I've been
since you said divorce and how
your words grew dark as the foal's
severed muscle, dried so dead
it looked like rusty barbed wire
jagged splinter
cougar claw
dog's tooth
until it was scraped bloody
salved, wrapped tight
immobilized.

Too old for stitching, my edges
years hard, skin shrunk back
everything exposed, I join
the shocked foal in the stable

good leg quivering, bad
bandaged against blow flies
whose burrowing larvae
might clean proud flesh.

"Nothing but time
will help a wound this old"
the vet says.
"Lucky the muscle's
not sliced clear through.

Whatever you do
    don't let him run."

Run?

A rivulet of red streaks down
from the bandage into the stall stench
and the mare will not be kept away longer.
I press my head against her sweaty flank
as the foal suckles away his fear breath.
Flies buzz. I feel the scrape of seconds.
I smell milky life in the minutes
in the scrape, scrape of minutes.

Before asphalt and concrete

I could have followed your dust
I could have run along
beside your horse
tasted the hard grit of your leaving
felt the needle-stings in my eyes
had an excuse for tears.

I would not have stood
camera in hand, snapping photos
of your departing Buick
the orange tarp covering
your belongings
in the luggage rack.

I would not have had to rush in
to your room with my white cloth
and lift the lint of your living
from every unyielding surface there.

If it weren't for all this concrete
and asphalt separating us
I could see the dust
of your returning
from a long way off.

Weatherwatch

I always watched Ohio weather
no matter where I was
to touch snow with you
see robins strut in rain

imagine your white handkerchief
pulled across your brow in a heat wave
and you in your gray suit
folding the ironed white square neatly
and placing it in your breast pocket
with a friendly pat, remember

how you tapped my cheek the same way
when we talked in concert
said "snap" and laughed until
we grew silent looking at each other
playing games in Ohio
what our daughter would have
looked like, how we would
decorate our home, cancel
each other's votes, argue
politics, grow silent
looking at each other.

Today it is hotter here in Oklahoma
104° of swelter. I run the sprinkler
to cool the wild bird I have raised
since a cat destroyed its nest.
I think of your room
and the stealth that crept in
late last Sunday morning
while you read the papers
in your separate bedroom
and died without me
in Ohio.

If a Tree Falls

Is it sound in the forest we do not stand in but believe?
Is it green, unwitnessed, fire in the absence of ash
the sear of love welding the feet graveside
the limping away to reluctant escape
hurrying to accounts of near-death experiences?

Is it sound when the acorn splits with spring
when buds burst through winter
and the leafless crocus
speaks in tones of yellow?

Is it a wife in the story
told without the man who dies
or is it something more
the arboreal standing alone
when one of the pair
of matched oaks at the gate falls
and grass begins to grow
in the unshaded place
like his beard still does?

Is it sound after the cleaning of closets
the picking-over of his things by relatives
or can it be sound
if it is a blessing in the forest
anointment in the garden
like the heat of childhood
like the silence
when we float
above ourselves?

Dogwoods in the dark

seem to be sleeping
like my bird
their heads tucked under
and their moon wings
feather puffed
and bloom soft.

Oh, the pale breast
of a spring night
upon what I love
upon what I've lost.

You leaving me
your light less
than moon bright now
my voice unable
ever to shake you
from profound silence.

How beauty drops
against the heart's angst
downy petals gathering
moon and moon
into my cratered grief.

This is how we leave life.
This is how life leaves us
a light leaping, sun
to moon, moon to earth
a sleeping, an underwing
breathing out of
our earthly selves.

When I Am Old

When I am an old woman
will you pluck the whiskers
from my chin, recognize
my eyes, faded blue
see to it I don't sit
widow's hump pulling me
into a fetal curve
                                        one
in a long row with
Mr. Mack protruding his tongue
from between the automatic doors
of his two lips, like a cuckoo
on schedule.

Keep me away from the old lech
across the hall, who tries to show
his private parts to us women folk
and the men too.

When I am old and pushed against
the wall with Maggie's non-stop wailing
and you walk down the corridor
where I have been positioned
don't dare pat my hand
or my head, or anything
of mine, especially my wheelchair
as though it were part of me. If
I've told you this story before
stop me.

**The Old Woman Says, Bring Me Garlic
and Grandchildren**

Something blooms that should wither.
A bell that should not ring tolls.
There is something supple and unbruised
which wants to flee like sprung green
from the coiled root.
I am hauled back and forth.
What is my name now that I have planted
and harvested, now that the seed of me
has sprouted and borne fruit? Who am I
bubbling in the stew pot—meat that is eaten first
the potato unearthed and boiled to softness
last of the soup thinned too much with water
oversalted for savor. Oh, bring me garlic
and grandchildren for my knee. Is this too much
for an old woman who eats alone to ask?

Sitting here on the porch, in sun
where the mud dauber collects spiders
and stings them to paralysis to store
for her young, I wait in my clay house
collect memories for hungry, red mouths
immobilized wisdom for sharp teeth to awaken.

I work on the painting in my lap
shave the dust fields of melancholy
from the canvas with a single-edged razor
until the nicked vein blooms blood
and arterial fountains pulse. This is not
the work of some pain merchant
vending old griefs, but release
of a tender sliver planted in my girl heart.

Bring me wild onion and cheek roses
the veined lids of sleeping children, bring

something that should bloom on my windowsill
something that will bloom after the bell is silent
something that will not be the color of anything old
something that is not remedy, but promise.

Jesus, My Special Effects Man

My bare feet grow uglier
from more than forty years
wandering in the wilderness.

I do not know if you are leading
following, or near Sinai
revising commandments
watching, while I remain locked
in the maze of some movie set
where Hollywood seems more credible
than God.

Have you left a silk thread
to save me from the Minotaur
or have you crossed the river
and returned changed?
Are you the special effects man
who rolled back the sea?

I search canyon rims for you
the yellow sky sour in my eyes
everything in silhouette
the pressed-flat film rolled
across the screen like
a long-awaited premiere
attended by invitation only.

In My Pocket

I am contemplating escape routes
how I would slide down the silk shoulder
of a golden Buddha in Thailand
or fugitive from Cuba, from silence
bounce over waves in a swollen rubber tube
miss Florida, but not regret Miami

maybe float by a shrimper, be rescued
from the Mississippi-mud Gulf
and arrive in New Orleans for Mardi Gras
plastic necklaces floating through air
rings of gem-spark on the sky's pool

when what I need most is a garden
like Monet's lilies
something so luminous
these rivulets of darkness
cannot streak across the canvas
breaking the ambient mingle of colors
into glass-hard islands
in an unnavigable sea.

In my pocket is a sextant
alive with the secret of light
and my shoulder bones project triangles
that could be sails, or wings.
My feet, mired in the tarry thickness
are shaping like rudders.

Landlocked, I snap green living
from a tree and waft it
over the rising dark
a trembling twig
dowsing for direction.

THE LAYING ON OF HANDS

she witched

with a sapling

for the water they drink

and her fingers grew knotted

like roots

Salmon Run

Somewhere three hundred twenty miles
above us all, astronauts take pictures of Earth
ornamental Earth, a lapis and opal brooch
solitary treasure, pinned on the black silk
blouse of space and reflecting the light
of continents, loose-mounted, side by side
brilliant against a burnished sea.

In the buoyant heavens space scientists
laden with the future and destination
float their experiments, turn base metals
into gold, pebbles into jewels.

Intrepid travelers
they wait for glow-in-the-dark
Earth bulletins to keep them company.
They listen to crack and whistle
messages hail them
from light years away.

They leap upstream
toward their origins
silver and sunlit
in the rapids of time.
They spill ruby roe
into the still pools
of grace.

Light Wells

Looking for a god
for all occasions
I read of
the opening betrayal
and apple demon
in a book of falling
called Genesis.

I read of the
small crucible of love
in Luke, how it was shaped
like a manger
and I wonder
was it made
of wood and nails?

I make pilgrimages, searching
for ancestral perspectives.
I hold the hand
of my wise father
and the hand
of my child-like mother
and listen.

They tell me
of myth eagles
malicious mirrors
and magic fields.
They give me
their unauthorized version
of the improbable.

We sit together in the A frame
they built and named
Gingerbread House
their place in the woods

where they watch birds
through the huge hole
they cut in the wall
without help from anyone.

A revolution in glass
they called it
old folks
doing it their way
lifting the patio door
to the second story, together
no fear of failure.

After all, she witched
with a sapling
for the water they drink
and her fingers
grew knotted
like roots.

He pruned and grafted
in his orchard
playing with life
until he had an enchanted
plum pear peach apple tree
for his grandchildren.

They have an alliance
of wings
in this abode
of light
where I drop
my bucket often
into the deep shining.

Birthday

Gray, like the wing-dust of moths
settles in my brown hair as I move
toward half a century of life
toward something that makes me
want to touch it like a newborn's head

to the place where the patterns
of my fingertips curve like raked gravel
in a Buddhist temple
                    and wait
in contemplation, upturned to the sky.

The soft child of me sprouts green
in the light bled from behind
my eyes, and my hands
                    wait
like a bruise healed to yellow
in the garden of my survival.

The soles of my feet harden
as I run with my kite
on Children's Day
when my raised hands
like rushing sparks leave
their imprint in the air
and the years
            are burning.

I want flight, / plenty and song before blindness, / then one mourner who will know / me by my colors, who will / preside at my burning / and be willing to change.

from "Retreat," by R. T. Smith

I will be the one mourner

who will know you by your colors
and at your burning be transformed
my subsequent geography
an atlas of light
a path through the labyrinth
of imagination
an escape from
the high hedge maze

and you, a summer idyll
garden of visions
garden of mystery
garden of grand design
of arbors and pavilions

of dreams—the blush rose
old fragrant roses, rambling
full-petaled peonies
fronds of royal fern
mulberry velvet pansies
secret garden.

Inside walls draped
with garlands of white wisteria
I will tread aromatic herbs
know yellow by the lemon verbena
I press between my fingertips
be healed by medicinal green.

Salvia will be the fire
of your going, its flame
moated by a watery
apprenticeship of sorrow
fallen tears
abundant as violets

their legacy enlivened
with orangeries
apricot
and apple
pairs of trees
alabaster statuary
fountains and lavender.

Garden
within a garden
you
Spring
in purple crocus
paper white narcissus
snowdrop and blue star scilla

in the pink burst
of plum blossom
above sun-dappled path
Spring
branched and leafing

a refuge for the red bird
of your heart
which inhabits
this winterless sanctuary
against the darkness
at its weedy edge.

Leaving the Women to Plow

I fall with my face toward the battle
drummed into earth by marching hymns
no longer willing to perpetuate the lie guns tell
and I imagine that when my horse wanders home
one year later, there will be mourning like the time
my playmate died of poisoning from eating jimsonweed.

My cheek rests on the soft prayer that clung
to my mother's lips, green and faithful as moss
and in the dreamtime when I am forgiving everyone
forgiving myself, I see my father's eye aimed
down the gun sight of the rifle he taught me to use
in self-defense, his pupil black as the barrel hole
mind loaded, heart cocked.

Something unsoldierly rises up in me, willing bull's-eye
and my fingers comb wild grass like they combed tangles
from my wife's hair. I breathe hard through the aroma
of blood and soil in my nostrils, bite my wet lips
and fall back to a weedy time, before jimson.

(for great-great grandfather Will Connally,
reluctant soldier of the Confederacy)

Baptized with Riddles

You guess at beauty—whether it is the peony
you hold so cupped on petaled life this dawn
or your hand disturbing the dewy web
which veils its prismed bloom.
And you ask questions
of truth's wash. Is it the flow
of first breath or its final ebb
the everyday death or
the everyday spirit?

You rise transformed
an astonishment of heart
clinging wetly
the grace of memory visiting
like one of the numbered
afternoons alone in the woods
when you said something aloud

just before the hawk silenced the birds
and all your syllables shredded
fell like dried needles of pine
until mute, you drifted, flotsam
in the slow current of your words.

What could you have spoken
to the radiant, how replied
to the white throats
piping their invitations
into the sinuous branches?

Before the unbuilt beauty
and unchiseled space
what could you have said
of love?

More light

brighter than the best answers
more warmth than memories
pressed against my eyelids.

Letting go of shadow, I see
Grandpa's smile in death's greening
when I was eleven

how he prayed to go in his sleep
got his wish, and made me angry
with his peaceful face

and my dog, asleep forever
on the glistened grass at dawn
in sunrise I ignored

the faithful neighbor's chow
nestled beside her, father
of her numberless pups.

You—you in a distant grave
year deep from my touch
your voice muted

you come to me
in the one bright cloud
of an evening rainstorm

more light
than I have
ever seen.

She could not make an ordinary noise if she tried.

Donald Hall, about Marianne Moore

Ordinary noises we don't hear

like night, the abyssal hunter
stalking the eternal food
no practice of the body
prepares us for, light

an *Om, Om*
meditation on gardens
or the unheard whir
of vermilion flycatcher
collecting leaves
hair, spider silk

or poets who witness to us
gathering light—messengers
with an appreciation of fire
and the endurance of ignorance, bards
armed solely with a thin, bright foil
in a no-gravity situation
where the only dense thing
is the sharing of secrets

ordinary ones, inaudible as hands
circling a clock face
somewhere near Madeira
secrets guessed at
like true north
on a confused compass.

We are beginning to make language
with signs that disappear

like snowflakes
on the other side
of warm glass.

We are discovering
the mastery of division
the triumph of unity
understanding the vague
whisperings of living rock
   a thousand legs of centipedes
                                        dancing.

On your birthday, which I thought was yesterday

because I am not attuned to calendars
and numbers lace through me
like snakes I am not afraid of
even today when I stop by the roadside
to gather hot peaches, near ripe
from limbs stretched across barbed wire.

I wish we had been children together
wish you could have told me
your imagined stories
and I would have believed
sitting in the tall weeds, hidden
from grownups, like now
when I stand in Johnson grass
rust seed heads swaying around my head
while I dream the best birthday gift
for you, an extended poem
that reads life-long and speaks
of peach tree leaf curved like lime slice
spotted yellow and speckled with brown dot eyes
like the sparrow hawk's that watches me
watch it, fuzz of warm peach in my hand
like a newborn's head, almost ripeness
reaching toward like my words
you pour light on. They open
to what I want to say
delicious as a stolen peach
eaten hot.

To forget is the great secret of strong and creative existences—to forget after the manner of Nature which knows no past and begins again every hour the mysteries of her indefatigable productiveness.

Balzac

Directions

(for when you can't remember
the mnemonic device)

Reach into your right or left brain
and retrieve the last word you said
to the first person you knew who died.

Calculate the approximate number of wrinkles
in your mother's face
by multiplying the furrow in her brow
and dividing by the number of smile lines
radiating from the corners of her eyes.

Recall the hardest goodbye you ever said
the first live birth you witnessed
the smell of a newborn. Imagine

what the Star in the East
really looked like. Contemplate
the beginning of time
the origin of man
and the meaning of life.

You won't forget
how different stars look
afterward.

How to Meet God and Remember It

Sitting in church, your feet dangle
legs not long enough yet
to be planted, clay-heavy
in the firmament of faith

the pew something to squirm on
your tongue not ready for wine or bread
your heart not ripe for thorn and spear
everything so fresh that your shoes
fascinate you for a while

until beyond the sermon
you hear children playing
and see through stained glass
the true color of fields and sky.

All the untasted titillates
and hungry as you are
you cannot sit still.
Your tongue thrashes
in its cage of little teeth
hands pick at Sunday best.

Your mother slips you a peppermint
takes your fingers from the button you twirl
holds your hand in hers. It settles there
nestles in down from her breast
sinks in soft feathery.
Your chirruping ceases.

She calms you, pushing back
the cuticles on your fingernails
releasing to the world
again the newness of you
a gentle birthing this time.

From the pulpit
pronouncements of God soar
like hawks diving
but she spreads her wings
over you
and feather by feather
you learn
a benevolence
you will never forget.

(for Millie Posselt and her mother)

Mother in the Mirror

The brush makes music in my mother's brown hair
pizzicato sparks fly into the dark beyond
the kerosene lamp. When she bends down
silk strands fan out to sweep the floor
before she captures them in a knot
high off her hot neck.

I watch her in the day, how she moves
when she does what she pleases
polishes the lamp chimney
polishes the mirror
weeds the flower bed.

At night my brother and I bathe
in the zinc tub after our father
in his milky water. He empties it
outside on her zinnias while she
sprinkles our bed with saved rain.
Her voice is soft.

From my bed I spy through my lashes
see my father bring fresh water
to fill the tub where she sits
knees tight to her. I smell the mint
she rubs on her arms, her thighs.

She is drying in the air in lamplight.
Water sinks into the plank floor
in front of the mirror. From their bed
behind the bureau I hear the soft rumble
of his voice in the dark, telling her
the day's news and machine-shop gossip.

The room contracts into a cameo
of mother in the mirror. Her fingers

light as petals, touch her lips
her cheeks, let down her hair.
It clings to her wet shoulders.

My eyes close. I have never seen her
wear a nightgown in summer. I cannot wait
to grow up. Even with the sheets sprinkled
it is too hot for clothes.

What You Can See in March

When you look through
the circle your hand can ring
you see a smaller sky, more blue
and the weathered gray peaks
of a picket fence, pointed
like jousting lances.

Crossed shadows of the rope hammock
make geometry lessons, framing purple clover
while a lone dove on the electric line
seesaws in wind.
Overhead, a sparrow on a limb
looks spectacular without its tree.
Nothing is ordinary when you can
hold it with your eye.

The winnowed world
falls in colored bits
between the mirrors
of your kaleidoscope
and memory turns.

Last winter's lone California Anna
hovers at the hummingbird feeder
accidental, blown across a country
and captured in the circle
you made on your
steamed kitchen window

stranger
sipping the nectar
of your hands.

Beyond the Kitchen Window

A woman wants a tree
her own leaves
trembling and dreamless

not trunk and branch
framed in a kitchen window
not a painting behind glass.

Something pricks her skin from inside
like new buds, and she wants to know
how leaves unfurl.

In spring she sees hail
scattered among severed twigs
like lost teeth of her children.

In summer she listens
to the noisy soil
hearing lessons of uncertainty.

She casts out her stone saints
in autumn and unroofs her house
with the slow scalpel of solitude.

Winter, and she abandons
the marmalade cat and roofless walls
survives snows of retribution.

Her branches beckon wings
which sprout spring plumage
of metallic brilliance.

Among the inhabited trees
a woman slow dances with wind
a woman who is a tree.

To be blessed

as though you had been mentioned by name
and could know the darkness that surrounds
not ignore it, but crouch under the down softness
of its weight with nestling heart racing
and naked wings stretched toward flight
eager for the and/or of life

to recognize your spiritual poverty, and not shiver
under the thin cloth of your experience
but bend with some photosynthetic wisdom
toward a resonant enlightenment

to watch the purple bruise of birth heal
and the creased flower of intelligence
burst through the sepal-tight fontanels
to envision its own demise

to be able to leave and go to an unvisited place
where only what you don't know has importance
where you cannot grieve what has happened
or never shall. There, fate is something
you leave outside, like muddy boots.

When you cross this threshold
there is neither in nor out
and to be motherless and fatherless
is not to be orphaned
but to be barefoot child
to squat by a stream's edge
and flow as fast as the unhesitant water
to wear the rough corners
of the world comfortably
and shape your self to everything.

Drinking Up the Twilight

This tasty cricket night
cicada moon
I have been buried for ten years
at the base of a tree
and now I rise, give off sparks
like fireflies at twilight
when I am on the bridge
listening to a song echo
in some undeciphered language
I don't need to know
to understand.
Here where the delicate weavings
of past and present
weigh lightly on my shoulders
like an autumn shawl
and the yellow years
twirl and spin, fall
like maple stars
in a floating spiral, I spin
spin under the cicada moon
in the cricket night
the air on my tongue
like spice, like salt
like new blood.
I am drinking up the twilight
crossing the bridge over the river
where stars float.
I whirl, I whirl
sparkler in the night
fire falling from me.
And in the morning
I see golden sprouts
at the base of a tree
and wonder what grows
here where I am.

Absolution

I'm a good-looking
ugly woman, not the shadow
of a great name, but issue
of an ocean which birthed a fish
discontent with swimming

and I have forgiven myself
for everyone I loved before you
the shoulds and should-nots
of a lifetime, all the nights
I waited under the beautiful star
explored some noble lie

wanting to explain the unknown
wanting to understand in order to believe
ignoring my heart which had reasons
my reason knew nothing of

and I have forgiven myself
for my children's bad manners
my bad back, the dog's escape
the dead battery when I left
the lights on in the parking lot

for the cave-in on my brother
when it was my idea to dig to China
the kiwi fruit I bought off-season
at its highest price and hid
in the egg compartment
so I didn't have to share.

I have absolved myself
for not flossing my teeth
every day. I'm lookin'
good.

Faith, Hope, and Mystery

I keep wondering where to find it in the ideological rubble
the distorted history and unresplendent solutions
whether to search the Rift Valley on a day divined favorable
or cover myself in ash and bathe in some sacred river

whether to follow faint luminaries to a problematic altar
or make my own heresies—carry the trident of war, death
and despair before me like an anecdotal warning
of the transitory nature of nature

or whether to search statistics for answers
recycle garbage, forego cholesterol
turn off the tube and read
begin listening, or stop

whether to claim my inalienable right
to pursuit, to the limp through galaxies
whether to assemble in the name of liberty
or life or resplendent human laughter.

Maybe they're rhetorical questions
She's finding faith, hope, mystery in joy

This is my hand

and nowhere in it will you find
a line so straight as the roof peak
a carpenter hones razor-sharp
against the tender face of sky.

It curves on your thigh
rippling like live oak roots over earth
hesitant before they divide into
thirsty fingers.

These lines know no hard angles
like corners—no wall or sharp division
where ceiling and floor break away
to more wall

but curves—like horses' necks
like beach, a French horn maze
of music spinning out in nonlinear
celebration of the unbounded

and everywhere I leave my fingerprints
miniature meditation gardens
to contemplate like concentric designs
raked in gravel beside Kyoto's Golden Temple.

I can turn this hand like wind turns in a storm
cup it to drink rain or let drops escape down its slope
like tears roll, round as wild persimmons

or my anger flees into the center of my fist
captured by carpal bones that bloom
when they open, sending messages
wafting out to return like echoes
seeking their source.

This hand of more
than five parts
how it fits the other
to make a church, a steeple.

Questions and Answers

Why
I look at your hands
and think they belong on a piano
see your door ajar and knock
trust my secrets to you.

Why
I believe most of what you say
don't avoid your eyes when we talk
believe you will not hurt me
when I know you could.

Why
I invent reasons you are what you are
question myself as to my curiosity
convince myself it is not important.

The answer is all in your laugh
like fingers dancing a Strauss waltz on a Steinway
or a door that cannot lock me in
threshold that can be crossed and recrossed.

It is in the laugh of your eyes
recognition of the floating joke
we swim together
hilarity of curiosity in an ocean
of no answers.

It is shared humor
at the makeshift sail we dream
before we have even discovered
a boat.

I had a glove

the night we danced
and you looked for the lost one
we laughed
when you could not find it
tossed the other
into the river
no, it was a stone
held in my hand
and sank to the earth's core
where precious metals signaled
follow the magma
and it rose, small scent
of woodsmoke on the air
twist of a cloud
in cicada summer; it was yearning
rather than a glove, it was
velvet on a hand, it was
a glove such as you have
never touched
fingers interlaced
like ivy, palm open
half-shell of an oyster
it was a pearl
beating on the pulse
at my neck

Which to Believe?

What if you should love me
and I should love you

or if I died thinking poetry
and you lived being the poem

or without my natural resistance to sleep
you would be my best dream

then the morning after I would leave
my insomnolent heart behind

take an axe to tree
despite having vowed never

to cut live wood except
for fashioning the finest violin

then you would become the hollow
where my chin rested

and the scrolled curve end
of an elegant neck silent with waiting

until the stroke of my rosined bow
sobbed and laughed to your ache and solace

until you took deep flight
upon a last tremulous note

and together we perished
in a poem.

THE PROMISE CURVE

the strange atmosphere

of quasars, pulsars, and love

antimatter and what matters

a speck of light

that leaps between your hands

How to Save a Soul

If you want to save a soul
play the part of primitive magician
indulge in the theater of mirror
and reflect the upstart gorilla
excelling in evolved folly.

Recount the exodus of the sacred
the Nile eclipsed, pyramids
returned to desert.
In the sand, portray
the afterlife of saws
when the last rainforest
has been felled.

Speak of the eye's catch-light.
Speak of other dimensions.
Etch the soul's grooves
with the music of forgiveness.
Give lessons in ignoring
the accident of face
and offer a reclaimed future.
Teach this soul to enter death
with the faith of seeds
and the miracle of doubt.

What Pulses in Stone

Writing a divination manual is a wild business
one to be pursued only after a life
beneath the forest floor you enter
through the cave of skepticism
knowing that light is imperiled
and you listen in solitude
as mushrooms sing for it.

When your ears are full, you scan the sky
for answers in the blue blueprint
and as you rise with the good stealth
of birds—of birds, rise to see
a disappearing heart carved into a trunk
and a blur of wooden architecture
on your way to the world of rival sages.

Where is your pen?
You are prepared to enter fire
into the pages, scribe an atlas in ashes.
The punishment of beauty drives you
toward a promise of grace
and you want to write a forbidden language
an explanation of circles.

In this book, rocks will speak
with the sweet throat of awe
and the parchment presence of souls
will be scribed with monastic loop and curve
an illuminated catalog of revelations will read
as untamed music, a contrapuntal hymn resound
attuned to the sun, and day leap its rhythm
over the heelstone, this lost book of Stonehenge
you want to write, this choir of granite
this symphony of megaliths.

Selected Poets

Leafing through
portraits of the poets
I see their eyes
a single flame
blown wide

consuming edible weeds
the animal/vegetable
inky ash of
Sheep Sorrel and Sowthistle
Coltsfoot, Goat's Beard
and Shepherd's Purse.

What they taste
mouthing their hearts
Honey Locust and Peppergrass
Wild Garlic, Sweet Flag
Persimmon and Sugarberry
their tongues in ears
the bitter wax of audience

being heard imperfectly
the shared penance
for imperfect utterings
Pokeweed, Arrowleaf
Spanish Bayonet
absolution in the hands
of an unpriestly public

the bardic pilgrimage made on naked knees
through Catbriar, Stinging Nettle
and Tumble Mustard
in search of the perfect word
for Jewelweed.

The hiss of space

is collecting in dishes
where we lap
star messages
like kittens.

Our whiskers
beaded with cream
we frolic
beneath celestial
collisions.

Ten billion neutrinos
pass through my
daughter's small finger
which touches a beetle
on the petal she bends to.

Particles in a cloud chamber
ricochet, contained chaos
and she makes language
from words which strike her
at random.

"Flower," she says
pronouncing a new cosmology
a quantum unfurling
in yellow dust
on her nose.

Cloning the Stars

With a backyard telescope
you introduce your granddaughter
to the night sky
    "look, Amanda
      through here"
you say, and point to the tiny lens
where she squints, but finds nothing.

You kneel beside her
cup her hands in yours
and in the afterglow
of the big bang
choose to clone
one sharp point of light.

Together, you collect
green and orange vapors
gather gold and ruby
press them into a sphere
ball them up with blue and violet
squeeze
squeeze the spectrum
into her delight.

Brightest Sirius glows
in your joined hands
scintillates in the strange atmosphere
of quasars, pulsars, and love
antimatter and what matters
a speck of light
that leaps between your hands.

Reunion

I name what I love
by its distance from me
soft names carved into marble
burning my eyes like pepper dust
sprinkled over the family stew in the iron kettle
every Independence Day, tasting sweet-salt
like the tomatoes Uncle Pearl grew, cool skins
stretched like birthday balloons
and Grandpa's leathery cheek I kissed
while he sat watching everything
his fingertips pressed together.

I breathe them all
the women's best aprons
spicy from cedar chests
their busy feet laying down the fine net
that held my world together,
cherry lattice pie of Aunt Sibyl
Aunt Mat, smelling of green beans
she cooked to brown
with bacon and new potatoes.

I see Aunt Grace afterward, smelling sweet
with her grandma bath powder, its velvet puff
and the ribboned, round box, apricot
her wet footprints stenciled dark blue
in the dusty linoleum after her bath
when I go back to the honeysuckle embrace
the room where her tub sits
on white porcelain lion's feet
and you can hear the night-singing mockingbird
serenade from beyond the porch where I sit
in moonlight, rocking, snapping beans
while they are still crisp and green.

The Connally Family Cemetery, Farm Road 27
Texas State Historical Site

The sun lights my father
where he kneels in the family cemetery
like an actor bound for destiny
plays him bright against the dark
backdrop of holly and bog myrtle
as he reaches to stroke
the pink granite headstone
of his most ancient ancestor.
Sunbeams play about his straw hat
until it glistens halo on his bent head.

My four-year-old granddaughter's hands
drift over carved letters
of our shared name, and I tell her
about my long-gone Grandpa
as she leans, hardly curious
against his cold, gray stone
under the shadow of loblolly pines
but she comes into my arms
when she asks about the tiny graves
Infant Phoebe, and no-name infant.

She asks why and why until I seek
the sunny space with my father
see him spiral up from kneeling
wild muscadine rising, his arms
tendrils looping around me
and his great-granddaughter
in the patch of light
and we walk together through shade
of cedar, oak, and hickory to a place
at the foot of his parents' graves.

The three generations of us stand
on the spot he says he wants to rest in

someday, and then we leave our departed
lock the gate, squint against the sun
walk our Cherokee walk across Peckerwood Flat
because of Cousin Richard's prize bull.

"Can we pick blackberries here?"
the youngest asks, already at ease
with the stare of the bull, and the sun.
"Along the fence line," Daddy says
"where no one mows them down
but you gotta look out for snakes
'cause it's that time of year."

Unaccountably moved to recklessness
the three of us plunge our hands
into the dark brambles
fill them with dusky berries
laugh at each other's blue lips
as we drive down Farm Road 27, forget
death and destiny, snakes and stones.
We taste the sun's ripe sweetness.
We relish it.

The Translucence of Flesh

The earthly luminance
around the borders of your father's face
like the light that pressed outward
from your firstborn
the gleam that left your eye
in bright abandonment

and now when he lies there
swaddled in white sheets
the radiant years shine
from his old bones.

See how the skin clings to them
pearlescent, tightly, like his hand
held your small one then
and yours holds his now.

Where is he going
with his smile
that makes you reverent
with his moonlight forehead

his blue agate eyes
his mountain range chest at dawn
his feet that have sown lightning
into the ground with each step.

Grandpa's Best Recipe

I find the other cure
(not the one for arthritis)
years after his death when I fall
on ice and need the battered cane
he willed me, find the cure
when I pull the worn cap
off the cane tip to exchange it
for the safety of a new one.

Grandpa's walked-miles drift from the old cap
in fine, gray powder, sprinkle me in a soft baptism
of revelation I rub all over my bare arms
whispering, "Dust of my grandpa," as Indian artifacts
he plowed up begin to rattle, and I can see
Grandpa's father Will and mother Susan in the tall grass
hiding from Caddo Indians, clinging to each other
until they reach East Texas piney woods, clear just enough
for family, leave the best untamed, like my wild father.

Two generations later, six years old and naked
he wages a bullnettle fight with his brothers, all lashing
and being lashed, then pissing on each other's wounds
and jumping in the creek for a cooling and catfish grabbling.
I can see cotton fluffed up in the field, the gathered corn
hams hanging in the smokehouse when Grandma dies
with my daddy ten years old and watching. Such dust.

But that was 1926, and a long time before Grandpa came
to live with us, rising too early to suit some
planting his orchard trees
and beans and squash and corn and okra
making up his arthritis recipe
of boiled oranges, grapefruit, lemons
the rinds too, and cream of tartar.

"Guaranteed to cure," he proclaimed
leaving the citrusy potion to steep
while he sat in his wicker chair
and watched wrasslin' on t.v., beating
the chair arms with his Bible-holding hand
in a fist, his healing-preacher hand
and shouting, "Kill 'em! Kill 'em!"
or flailing his cane in the air
when he was all tuckered, hollering
at me and my brother and Sugar dog too
  "I'm gonna break every bone in your body
   if you don't stop pesterin' me."

But Sugar never flinched, just followed him everywhere
like I did, his cane pointing to the Alberta peaches high
on the trees he had planted when they were puny
whippersnappers like me, or poking with it at new seedlings
 "They'll amount to somethin', little sprout
  if we keep the weeds out, leave the bugs
  to the birds, and trust in the weather"

which he didn't, but he loved the risk
leaning on that cane, it sinking into the soil
it picking dust up off a paved road that last day
when he thumped in the door red-faced, muttering
 "Consarned doctor, don't know the meanin' of money
  expectin' me to take a taxi when it's not even
  five miles to home, and I still got my legs."

Picking up the dust, years down from the buggy
he used to drive to town and the plow he followed
the dust I could never wash off once it covered me
and sank into my memory bone
Grandpa's last best recipe
steeped in time and guaranteed to cure.

Where the Tongue Sticks

This is the year I touch buried memories
with gloves that are still wet on my hands
like the five a.m. dew, weed-chopping mornings
in Grandpa's orchard, mornings that surprised
falling like peach petals afterward into the crease
of my schoolbook, into the pleats
of the second-hand skirt I wore to Grandpa's funeral
the one that embarrassed Mama, whose fruit breasts
fed me first, my mouth brushing against things

turning blind to whatever was warm
Grandpa's coffin Daddy cried into
gripping the edge, which was lip high to me
and my tongue moved along the metal, slid
until it came to the place
where his hands had not been and stuck
on the cold, like my brother's tongue
on the ice tray, leaving little polka dots
of flesh on aluminum

in the dark church
where my father remembered
the morning of his mother's highest breath
when she became smaller than he had ever seen
smaller than a ten-year-old boy
and went deep into feathers she had plucked
for her last bed, moved forever from her youngest son
from moth-whisper of long cotton skirts, stiff coveralls
work shirts, the muted voices of his older brothers, sisters.

"She shouldn'na had 'im, never was the same after"
they said, and he moved to the room's cold edge
lit a candle in her honor and began to burn the long anger
that sustained him while he grew to elevate all women
pamper his daughters, spoil his wife, in defense

of the fluttering accusation that circled and circled
the light of his mother's bed in the single room

where she sank down far from the mourners' rail
my father and I filed past to the hard pews
his tears making diamonds in the wrinkles
of his creased skin, drops falling onto our
clasped hands like blessing I took later

cold salt wafer on my tongue
at the graveside where we stood frozen
like bits of flesh while Grandpa sank down
smaller than I had ever seen him.

Grandpa knew how to eat spirit

how to find transcendence
in the phoenix eyes
of his old Labrador.

In a snowblind world
he made his own horizons
sundreaming and warm
blessed with himself.

I walked with him, stole looks
at his Buddha smile, named him
sage   bridge   northern lights
    beloved companion

who gifted me with the bright coin
of love and death, a coin I keep
shiny in the velvet pocket
of my leaping soul.

My face is age-carved now, like stones
from the Monkey Temple of Kathmandu
        Om Mani Padme Hum
I find peace and good fortune
animated in my smile.

Should I Be Out Watching Whales ?

Should I be out watching whales
watching God roll over in the Pacific
his belly glistening, his great triangular
fin waving Trinity, his blow hole
saying, you too can breathe water.
Step into my wake.
Knowing whales do not
breathe water but filter
the best from it
and swim on, should I
here at the altar
still want to stand
and be baptized with
something more
than a sprinkle
something more
than leftovers
something like
an exhalation of
breathed water
should I still
want to
walk across
waves and
hear Him
breathing
wetly,
you
you
?
?

The Launching

I christen thee
    Certainty
certainty of hazard.

Blessings on the outspread cloth
whatever direction
the winds may blow.

Running free
close-hauled
or near-capsized by day

may you have calm nights
a beckoning sea breaking
mornings at your bow.

Deep the keel
of your darkest
imaginings

tall the mast
which pierces
the blue fabric of dream

sweet
the tuning of sails
to music's breath.

Bless the baton of rudder
the orchestra
of man and craft and sea

rhythm, rocked
into the bones
and sealed in salt

forever fresh the lust
of wandering, the yearn
for destination or no destination

the symphony
of celestial and nautical
where boundaries fade
compass to sextant
north to south
up to down

this hazardous place
the solo voyage of risk
the swinging boom, coming

the melody line
of this body
of water

this vessel
this man
in perfect pitch

the vibrato hull
captained by the percussive heart
and Neptune with his trident, blessing.

Multiple Epiphanies suitable ending title

We swim at midnight, map the sea
beneath the sea, navigate
with the sextant of light.
Back on board, we shake
the depths from our flesh, know
for sure we have come from stars.

The ape of history cannot haunt us here. history is huge
We have the endurance of eagles.
We are learning the natural history of wings. flight metaphor
Nothing seems unnatural—the deck underfoot
weathers pitch and roll as though appreciating history
such travel were ordinary for trees. not forgetting it all, bu
learning from it

Jumping land on the horizon
grows smaller in its ecstasy dance
and a riddle of hands
coils the anchor rope.

This flight before the wind
must be like the silence
after the big bang
this going, the vocation
of all our secret lives.

We thumb through books
wordstruck, knowing
there must be a sermon
in each letter of exultation.

We are not afraid as opposed to before - comforted here
to arrive at the last star
or read the final moon
like a compass.

There is a heavy flowering
of abandonment in our wake
and we have developed
the appetites of heretics
our debts paid in salt.

We have passed the danger zone
of solitude and latent lunacy
and we can read together
from the book of Earth
exchanging death's rasp
for the legacy of threshold.

This is the day before Creation
and we are in the beginning
sharing epiphanies
and wishing each other
journey mercies.

ABOUT THE AUTHOR

born in San Antonio

Kennette Harrison received a Master of Arts in English/Creative Studies from the University of Central Oklahoma. She has taught high school in the United States, Okinawa, England, and Scotland. Her experience includes editing *New Plains Review* humanities journal, and writing reviews, interviews, articles, essays, poetry, and a play. Her chapbook, *Kitchen Without Precedent,* won the Spanish Moss and Silences Competition, sponsored by Curbow Press, Georgia.

Her work has appeared in literary magazines such as *Poem, Cumberland Poetry Review, Nimrod Awards X, Southern Humanities Review, Prairie Schooner, ByLine, Negative Capability,* and *Black Warrior Review.* Anthologies such as Papier-Mache Press's *If I had my life to live over,* and scientific and historical journals, including the Native American publications *Changing Winds* and *American Indian Culture and Research Journal*, have published her writing.

Although firmly rooted in the mythical and real Texas of her birth, Kennette began a nomadic life early in her career when she taught in Okinawa with Department of Defense Overseas Dependent Schools. From her beloved East Texas piney woods to life in foreign lands and her home in the Oklahoma countryside, she has written grounding poetry which is a quest for faith, miracle, or illumination—a quest not laden with dogma or heresy, but a buoyant, spiritual journey.